DECADE OF THE BRAIN

POEMS

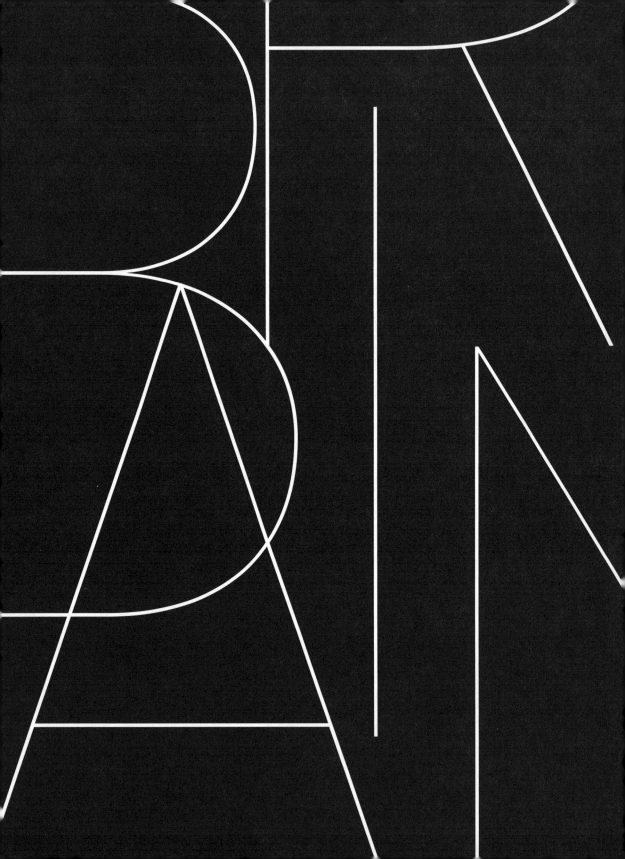

JANINE JOSEPH

DECADE OF THE BRAIN

POEMS

Alice James Books
NEW GLOUCESTER, MAINE
alicejamesbooks.org

CELEBRATING 50 YEARS OF ALICE JAMES BOOKS

10 9 8 7 6 5 4 3 2 1

Alice James Books are published by Alice James Poetry Cooperative, Inc.

Alice James Books
Auburn Hall
60 Pineland Drive, Suite 206
New Gloucester, ME 04260
www.alicejamesbooks.org

Library of Congress Cataloging-in-Publication Data

Names: Joseph, Janine, author.
Title: Decade of the brain : poems / Janine Joseph.
Description: New Gloucester, ME : Alice James Books, [2023]
Identifiers: LCCN 2022034175 (print) | LCCN 2022034176 (ebook) | ISBN
    9781948579308 (trade paperback) | ISBN 9781948579391 (epub)
Subjects: LCGFT: Poetry.
Classification: LCC PS3610.O6688 D43 2023 (print) | LCC PS3610.O6688
    (ebook) | DDC 811/.6--dc23/eng/20220721
LC record available at https://lccn.loc.gov/2022034175
LC ebook record available at https://lccn.loc.gov/2022034176

Alice James Books gratefully acknowledges support from individual donors, private foundations, the National
Endowment for the Arts, and the Amazon Literary Partnership. Funded in part by a grant from the Maine
Arts Commission, an independent state agency supported by the National Endowment for the Arts.

Cover art: Eden Some, A4 Original Studio Modern Abstract Ink Wash Collage, 21cm x 29.7cm. edensome.com

for J

She'd given you an impossible task:

she said to follow and you intended to.
But you'd come to a place in the forest
where there weren't any tracks—

BRENDA HILLMAN, FROM "FIRST TRACTATE"

My method to remember (the route) is identifying the two or three main rest points,
and repeating the moves between them like a poem.

ORIANE BERTONE

CONTENTS

)(

)(

)(

)(

)(

)(

)(

)(

)(

)(

)(

)(

)(

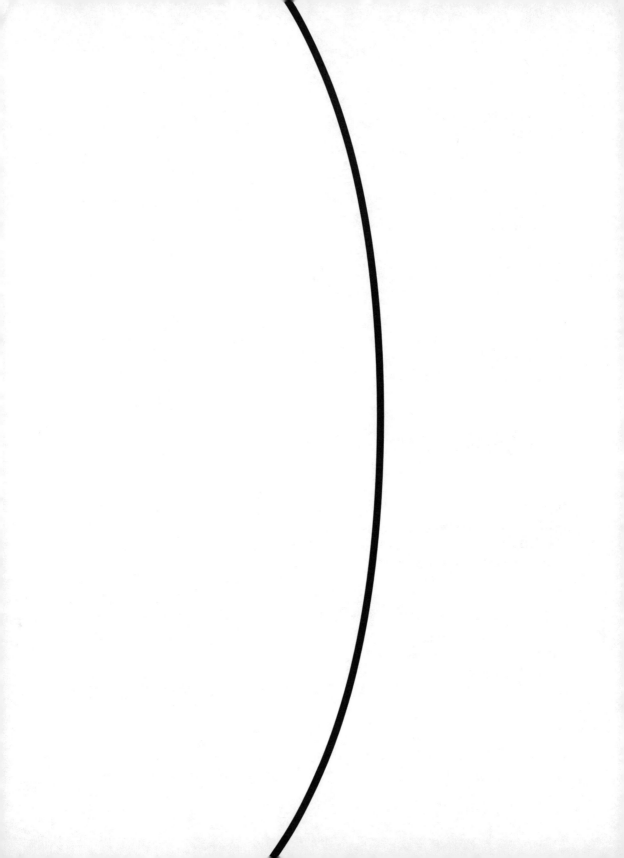

COUP-CONTRECOUP

I was at a low ebb when the ambulance

reversed along the gravel and the roar

traveled to Janine. For days the churned

rocks looped their sound until her brain

felt like the surf and the familiarity lulled

her to sleep. Lulled her in the hospital's

machines, lulled her in the backyard

of her father's home where she swayed

in suspension like the empty hammock

at first, then thrashed in the gale

like Odysseus lashed to the mass of me.

She could not tell you where I was though

the depths were in her. Wailing where

I waited were the sirens skirting the corner,

the vehicle still leagues away from rescue.

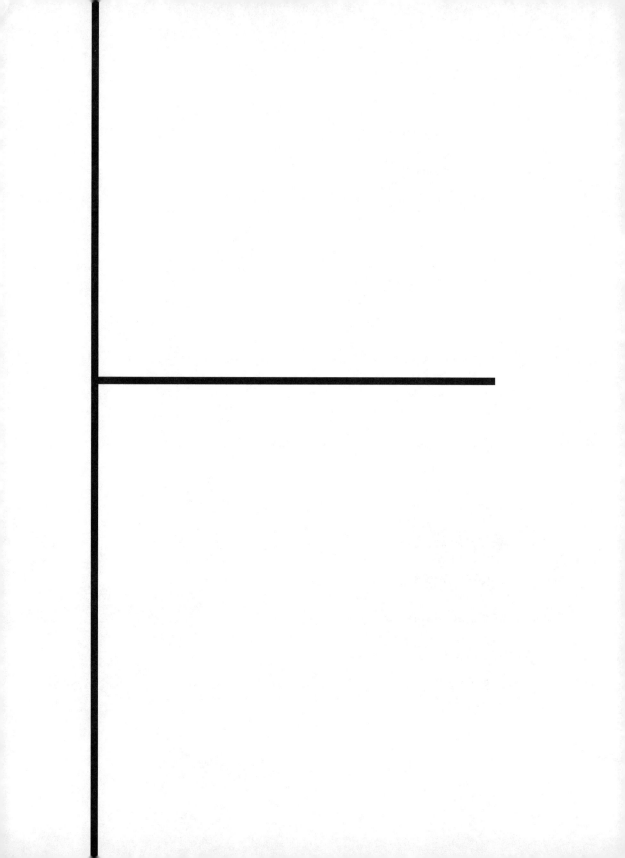

INTO THE GANZFELD

With my grief counselor I talk about hallucinating,

as a child, a double on the dashboard and my double
would say, *Don't you say a word*,

though I'd already be looking past myself
and at the horizon of taillights reddening.

It is possible to have been this way even then.
Even then it is possible something split in me

the first time I lied myself a citizen.
At the tilt of a head, was I the young woman

or the old, the duck or the rabbit in the optical
illusion? After the accident I turned out

all of the lights in the room while I watched,
concussed, from the mirror. I edged like a fever

with nothing on the tip of my tongue.

SELF-PORTRAIT AROUND THE BENDS

December 2008

    Not the light turning red or the back windshield

                              bursting in air,

               but that we could have died in a blue named Blue.
                                                                    Pearl.

                  Over an empty socket, the trunk's lid opened.

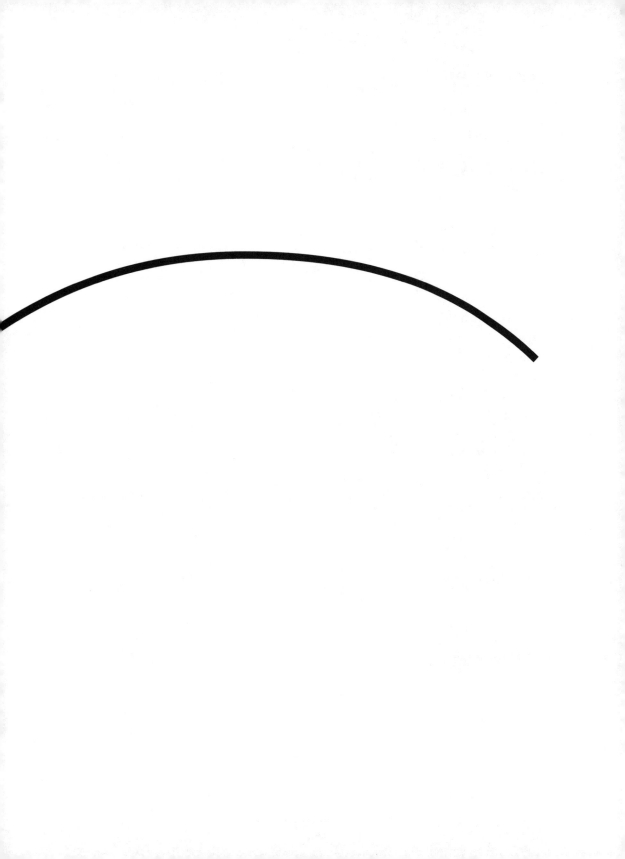

INTAKE FORM

In the beginning, there was a window

I pried the blinds to make light
of my losses

I fished my hands into and shattered
the water

What a hook I was

doubled in the beginning

In the beginning   My mouth

and the gasp upon impact
The skull intact

and the brain increasing
activity where the neurons

didn't die

Slowly I filled the form

X
X
X

My torso scored in order
of severity

only a diagram

FOUR DARKS IN RED

after Laura Jensen

Bad body is a hemorrhaging Rothko.

It drags like a laundry sack smearing

its unshowered oils across the wood floor.

Down the hall, bad body takes a break

like a bone. It balances its head

with a throbbing. Bad body complains

even the wind hurts. See how its hairs

rise when you get too close—

you are a zap of static. Bad body is so

negative. Bad body won't get dressed.

It stands in the open hallway

refusing to lift its arms for the shirt.

Refuses to lift its legs for the shorts.

Bad body says maybe tomorrow.

Bad body says can't you see I'm fatigued

in red and redder and black camouflage.

Bad body says don't move, just listen,

just stop, wait a second, give me

a second. Bad body swells a bad grenade

brain, cupping now its ears from the pealing.

HOW TO EXPLAIN MY BECOMING

another person?

In every shell I heard myself chasing
my brothers on a bicycle, the street and house-

lights blacked out as I trailed, water

rushing into my hollering mouth.
I listened

as my feet sank deeper into the sand pulling out.

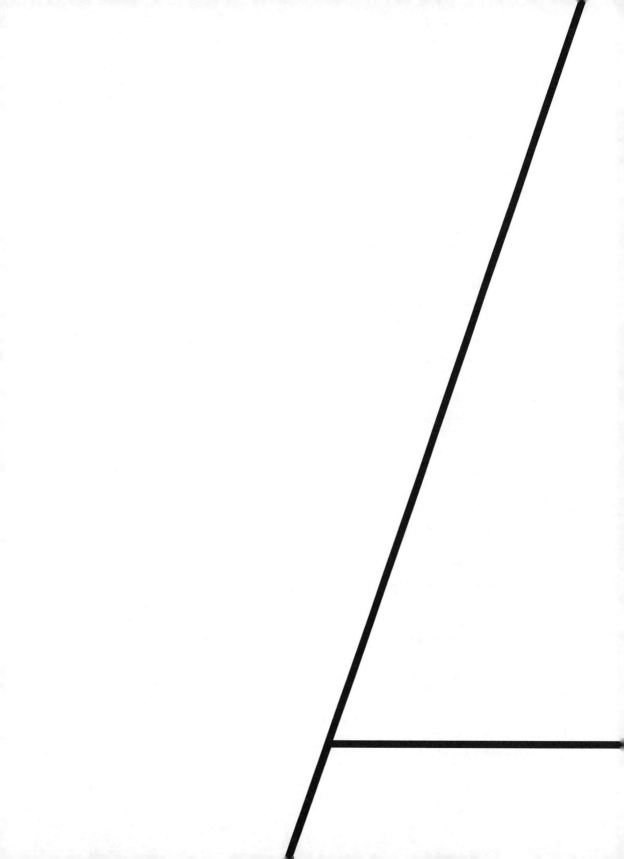

CIRCUITRY

I.

The rung wide
        receiver forgets why

he set his keys on the football field.
        Whose are they? he asks—a ringing

in his ear—while clenching
        the green. As if on the edge

of a pool, he tilts his head to drain
        water out of his canal.

It was like that, all the time,
        after. *How many fingers?*

he was asked, and not to tell
        a lie—it would mean his career.

It would mean recognizing you
        without your jacket when you

walked out of the room. It would mean
        you could say, *Stay here*

with me, and in his eyes
        could watch him come back.

II.

I spiral the parking lot, singing,
        It's alright, I'm alright,

while I count the pole lights back
        to my car. I practice *red, table, lamp*

with a neuropsychologist and now
        I can tell you about how my brain

blew in the acceleration. I was in
        a locked position—the details

unbearably clear in the replay and, still,
        no one else heard me swallow

the impact. Bend at your hips
        from your two-point stance and, there,

the muffler is a finger wagging
        one one one inches from the ground.

The tire-less car rests on its crutch
        of blocks, the windows a crunch

of glass. Are you feeling the rush now
        as you look to me, your brain still

in your head—is it still in your head?
        Can you point for me where

it happens in the connection, where
        on the line the old equipment

resets itself and loops?
        Is what you say the truth?

EVERY GOOD BOY DOES FINE

I aimed the lemon bar and pitched it.

I framed then flicked—our photos from the wall.

I slammed the door. Edged the Jersey barrier.

I'm sorry. My wrecking hands,

I explained. My head of wanting to

—wanting to, I couldn't explain. I said, Understand

I understand how someone could—.

I couldn't explain. So we could laugh, I called myself

The Incredible Hulk.

But I wanted to boil a bath to kneel into. Me and the laughing bubbles

bursting discordant. I wanted my childhood of rice to kneel onto.

I couldn't explain. *Keep a Gratitude Journal*, they said.

I confessed—told them as a child I selected the weapons of my punishment.

Told them about the armoire of buckles and wood.

How once all night I was punished out.

How once all night my temperature dropped by the pool.

How then the coaches at school knew what to do with my body

built to take a blow and put me on the field

on defense. *Get plenty of rest*, they said.

What if—, I said. On a loop,

What if—. What

hell was hel-

ixing in me, no one could say.

In the book I read, a concussion walloped its wife, then swallowed its hammer.

I roosted alone

in a loft with hardwood floors and floor-to-ceiling windows.

From everywhere in it you could hear me expose the bone.

I DO NOT LOVE YOU

What was it that you had said?

It came back to me, the book I split
      in the air. I was sitting on my stairs

when it came back to me: you saying you
      wanted me on the phone.

Who did the saying at my ear?

The walls of my apartment
      were domestic red. *Say it again,*

I had said. That's what *I* had said.

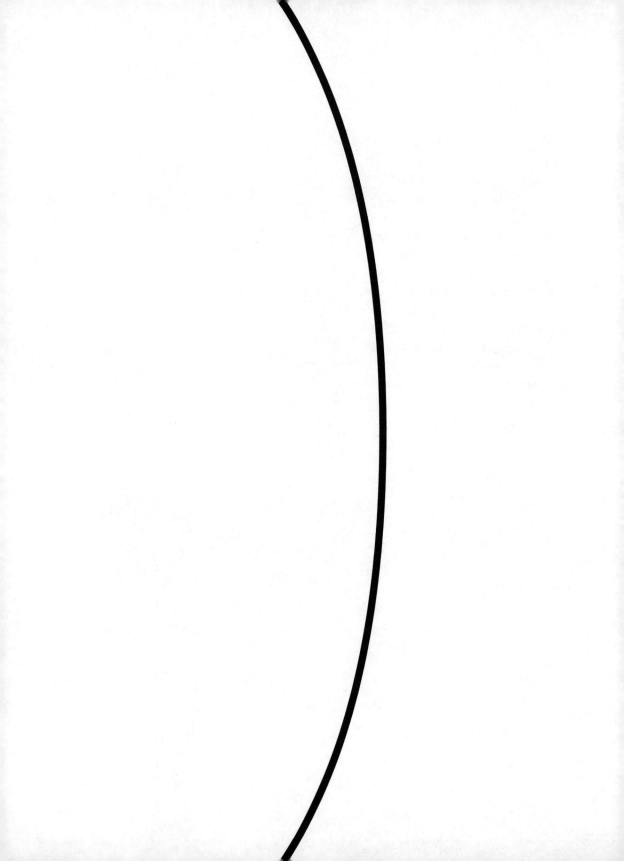

ERASURE

a Burning Haibun, after torrin a. greathouse

Re: JEANNINE JOSEPH
XXX XX, 2010

History: The patient is a 27-year-old, right-handed female. Two weeks ago on the 19th of May she was at the gym. She began feeling nauseous and nearly vomited. She walked out to get some air but noticed spots before her eyes, her vision seemed blurred, the room color seemed different and she developed a right-sided headache. She took a break, walked over to the student health clinic, went home and after a nap all of her symptoms had resolved with no medications or interventions. She has never had a previous episode such as this and no problems since.

She does have "regular headaches" frequently that are mainly a tension type headache in the base of her neck that can last days at a time but generally do not require medications. She uses an orthopedic pillow and massage.

In 2008 she was involved in a motor vehicle accident in which her vehicle was rear-ended. She apparently suffered a concussion at the time, was seen at XXX where CAT scans and subsequent MRI was negative. She then flew back to her home in Houston and had been followed by Dr. XXX and physical therapy for a year or so until she was released. She complains of being tired during the day, falling asleep during class, forgetting a lot, repeating herself. She gets lost. She switches words typing, has word recognition and spelling problems and cannot multitask. If she overworks her brain she says her brain "stops connecting" and she has to nap. She is however completing her PhD in Literature and works as a counselor *[sic]*.

JEANNINE

The patient

feeling nauseous   She

noticed spots   her vision

blurred the room   a   headache

a break

frequently   a tension

her neck   days at a time

2008 she was   was rear-

ended   suffered a concussion

She complains of being

asleep   forgetting   herself.

lost   switches

her brain she says her brain

16

She began feeling
She apparently suffered
She is however

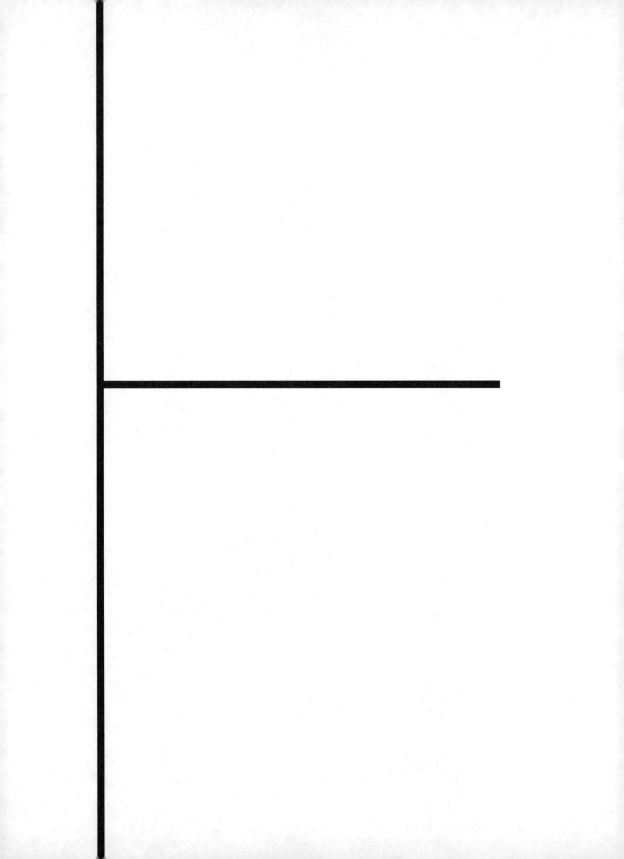

THE SPECIALISTS

For the commotion in my cranium, he relaxes me around the needle.
There-there, my trapezius twitches. I fasten my shirt across a constellation.

Almost there, he says, when I am *with at least partial improvement*. He circles
his desk to complete my patient history: *Subjective complaints of memory loss*.

Correct your posture, your position at the computer—there your brain will
follow. At home, I fell the foundation of me. *If I build it*, I quip, *it will come*.

Pressed to the drop table, my right contact slides from my eye, sticks there,
to my hair, like dew. I, too, condense to liquid every time he adjusts me.

There I keep no memory, so I move states. One specialist in the range
dampens my tinnitus by going, with her index finger, through my mouth.

He cups my head in his hands. He asks to know what it is like there, where
I'm from. *But I guess you don't tan if you're a colored*, he slips, then clicks my neck.

My notions scatter like mice when she strikes the singing bowl, trails two
kyanites up my spine. I quiver their current in me, a Frankenstein monster.

TELL ME OF PARADISE

I.

It is true; I was *ching chang chong*ed out

of the mountains where I made a home out
of my house. Out, out, out

I stared, an armchair toward the wall

with no hatch but a plan. So hell-bent I was, I—
with my head—took out a door.

II.

It is true; she was not seeing me-me, but me

doubled, doubling, sharpening as her voice
turned, secret discharged like a curse.

But what really did it, between you and me,

was when in her face I saw the peril
of my face come into focus.

She leaned on her elbows, then teetered

from the stool her full weight on the bar's table
to say, *This must be between you and me.*

III.

I hear the seeds I planted are birds now.

When upwards you walk to her home higher
on the street where once I lived, you must

tell me of my old front garden craning

perennially in her direction. Oh, you must tell
of the siege of beaks I fed manure and blood.

AMERICAN SENTENCES

I went first into the darkness to see what stars in this landlocked state

looked like from an Adirondack incline. A goblet of whatever

wine stalked alongside, then its tumbler: following to aid my eye in

the eyeing of the spectacle. He had the goggles and so beheld

at his red dirt's edge his pointer finger, each constellation's limit

elided with another's as he slurred. The lights in his assembling

twisted whale, crow, queen, even the crane to rat to rat to rat to rat—

mischief above and *colony* below. *As you would know,* he to me

turned. The screen door rasped behind us, so I made to move and moved once more

—once more into view. The others emptied from the kitchen and, under

the decorative illumination of the porch, made clear conver-

sation. All of us now, but none to vouch as he angled, *I know your*

homeland's run with them, into my remembering ear. Was it *over-*

run with? Or was it *ruined* with? My memory has clotted the ire.

Who's to say now if it was *Get out of this country* or *Get the fuck*

out of this country that he hitched an octave higher, yet no one heard.

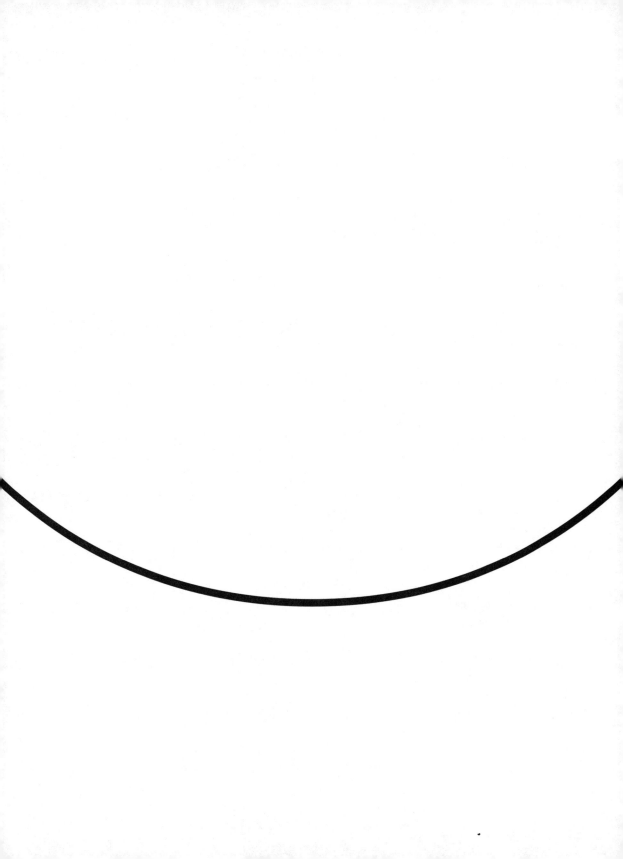

YOU LOSE YOUR KEYS, TOO, AND

believe a tenor sings
in your canal. You wake

one day midday and cannot

snooze the tuba, coiled trumpet,
now accordion flexing

its worm in your ear.

You cause a racket
up and down the building

and into the closet when you fall

as you stoop to lift
your basket of chores.

The door it drummed

on the rail, you relay
to the doctor, though you

could not hear it, or could not

hear it in your left, maybe
it is the right. You say,

I seem still

to be confused, your words
balanced in front of the other

and the other like feet,

so she conveys you
in a tube and says there can be music

if you cannot withstand the pulse.

LOVE, ELIZABETH

for E. K.

Their tittering,
        I heard, through

the tinnitus.
I pinched

    myself into the cluster,

        chuckling at your
    unbecoming, un-
professional, em-

    barassing valediction
        that I could not,
    for the dizzying

glare of the screen,
        read. I could scarcely

        remember why I was

    anyway in the lounge
or then down
        the hall when you burst

        through the double glass
    doors—a hiss
in the air from the air—

    to check in on
        me. *I think I have been*

in an accident,

I whiplashed fresh
        to you. Where your
                blood was pooling

        into a strip
from brow to nape
        you showed me,

                and said, *Oh,*
        I know, and in the space

we sounded ourselves

        like keyboards clacking
                or lettered dice around
        a grid, rattling and never

settling.

JANINE VS JANINE

after Spy vs Spy

Who were you at first I did

                      not know But in my prowling

speed I leaned my foot then car

              *

                      Flash I went and right you shad-

owed You then me then you then

                      me then me Out the corner

of my sight you fluttered Turns

                      we took ahead along the

feeder

              *

            Shook the cart I sensed

                      you merge Curved the aisle with snea-

ky wheels No one heard me hear

                      you whisper *Duck* I said and

dare you vanished In my ears

                      I stuck my fingers Mini

missiles zero danger

              *

          Spied

                    you in the convex mirror

As I paid you mouthed the words

                              Tapped my nerves like Newton's cra-

dle Trembled sweat I went to

                    pay *Wait* you said but no one

asked *Wait* you held but no one

                    asked

                    *

                    Hide you rushed I nearly

quickened *Lie* you warned inside

                    your bushel *Pass* you cracked a

metered accent Months you skulked

                    from impact trauma

                    *

                                        Tried a-

gain you choked me dizzy *Who'll*

                    be there I started asking

Rate my heart the light it ham-

                    mered Held my card to keep me

steady

                    *

          Who was I but sur-

                    faced from you *Safe* I said *We*

are each other Papers I

                    said *could mean tender* Same you

crept atop my shelter Watch

                    you kept a secret rooster

                    *

                                                        29

Wrecking ball you swung away

                  File in cake you knew the se-

quence Ambush on the desert

            island Club in branch you knew

was there

                *

        Useful you now flash

                within me Poles of me who

make the future *Safe* we hoot

                an alien's banter Dis-

tant we clap sounds like thunder

THE PERSISTENCE OF SYMPTOMS

During the short sale I moved my desk toward Charlie's
so that every day, when we came back from work,

he could say, *It's not even your house*, to my face

when I'd fret, *I can't lose another thing.*

Most of what I owned was slopped in return boxes
from other states and when I visited home

I complained about how I ever slept on that twin,

how my father couldn't even dust the venetian blinds

once in a while. It was the sixth or seventh house
I'd lived in, and not even one I'd say I grew up in

—I'd say the neighbors maybe found us eccentric

with the trellis heavied by wind chimes and roots invading

the porch's foundation—so he was right
to put the noise-cancelling headphones I gave him

back on while I agitated the sink. But it was our house

for a while, the lawn tended, the gnomes in a collection,

and before I used it as storage, I worried in it
about changing the motion sensors and whether

the leaky faucet was drowning the persimmon tree

my late grandmother and late beagle loved.

Charlie replied always with concern
about my googling old addresses again.

No one hated sentimentality more than I,

but when I flew back to consolidate my boxes,

I didn't know where to start.
Crayons, a below-zero sleeping bag, so many albums

of things I couldn't place. My things and what were

not my things. I circled trash bags around me

in the garage and tuned the radio in tears.
Just like that, it was for weeks. Inspecting frames,

books, dishes—separating what was not broken from

what was, dumping when I knew the difference.

NEAR THE END OF OUR TIME,

she asked me to imagine with her

        that it was as if—and I closed my eyes,

knowing where her sentence

                would twist. My faulting in the year

meant I could draw a shroud and visualize

        —not *nothing*, exactly, but nothing

on or *of*, say, the seaside
              in the relaxation exercise. Sheep bounding

clockwise to bedtime would

        subduct at my lids' shutting, my mind's eye

as occluded as the furred

              face of a Blacknose. I couldn't conjure

my toes to curl, a foot, my feet, an entire

        right arm, a fist to clench. *Relax.*

Open your mouth wide

              enough to stretch the hinges of your jaw,

read her sheets at home where I gaped

        between sessions, as cavernous as a casket.

IN THE ECOTONE

2019

Only when and only when I
                              develop heart palpitations—wake
as if undead from sleep—
                              do I remember being motioned
by wand from the mass
                              arms akimbo through security

As we were split into different
                              lines I said to my father en route
to take his Oath of Allegiance
                              See you on the other side
as he was quickened
                              out then out of sight

I observed the room as not
                              a room but an exhibition hall
an arena of partitions
                              as it with thousands that morning
in September across the news
                              tumefied with family and friends

Behind me someone *Years ago*
                              said *You could stroll right*
through without procession *Without*
                              this wait my god—
You just showed up—so
                              so great we got here when we did

My metals unfastened and
                              conveyed I crossed Janine
beneath the detector's flat arch
                              and appeared again Janine
without alarm or search
                              in the same fluorescence

Wholly I walked but imagined
                              I fizzed or interfered made a sound
like static between stations
                              or my body like a hologram
on the sensor threshold zigzagged
                              coming in and out then clear

What possessions I gathered
                              from the belt were pulsed though
with waves and until I was signaled
                              elsewhere I found myself lost
looking with familiarity
                              at the slate-gray flooring

It was of a shade similar
                              to the teeming lot on which I stood
when I eight years before became
                              a new American alone
who renounced and renounced
                              but did not in me feel the difference

I had for a time been from
                              form to form to form
unaccompanied in my ascent
                              so had supposed for a spell
I should for the duration also
                              as they say *go at it alone*

What did I remember of driving
                              homeward back to work
after my naturalization but myself
                              in my car dashing
singly like lines on the road
                              reflecting in perpetuity

I lingered in the echo until
                              like a shield I was moved
next into the atrium where
                              from a distance scored
yellow with caution tape
                              my father raised and flagged his arm

And until the court with a flick
                              fell dim we could see him
make with his fingers the sign
                              of peace meaning *two* as in
And then there were two or
                              as in *And now two more*

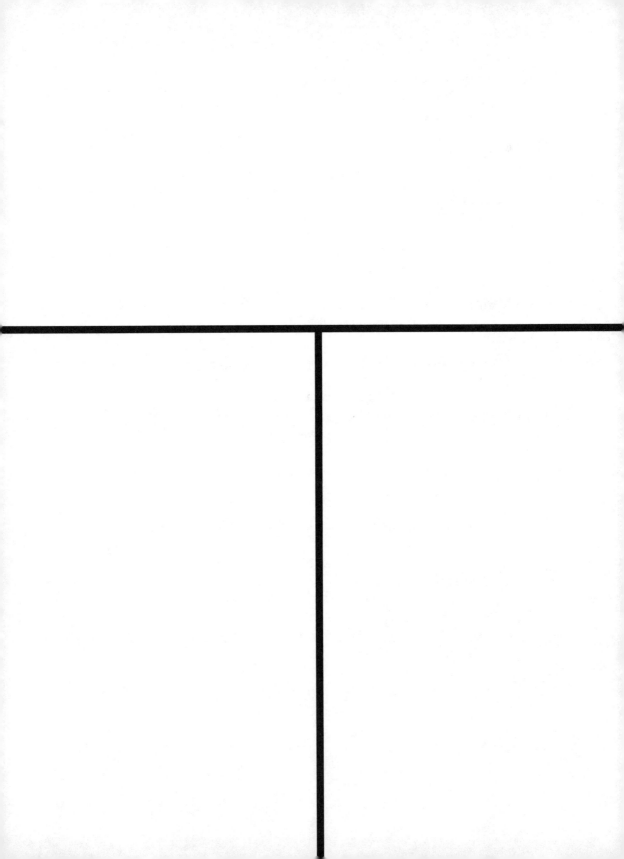

SPELLED LIKE *CANINE*

About my hair falling out, no one can do a thing.
        Weekly, the specialist needles my back

spasms so my bones don't sunder. I slacken after
        over ice—a happy hour. But my jaw,

when I roll in bed, clamps and fights the pillow-
        case into slits. I crack two and an eye-

tooth when the dentist finally swivels his arm
        into my mouth and resolves I need

a night guard. Hard, unlike the gummy ones
        I donned the years I socked around

the ring for fun. *Hard*, he says, for the gnash he
        can see when I unclench in the seat

though no one holds me. My ears don't fear the burr
        as he contours my ridges plain, so he

gallops his fingers quick to fit the tray. Mold in
        my maw, I seize and sip my breath

until we are done though no one holds me down.
        Nights now my incisors shift and days

my chew clicks, sorry
        I am not for the impression I bit.

INDELIBLE IN THE AMYGDALA

But during frightening situations—such as a car accident or a robbery—another area,
the amygdala, also lays down memories along an independent, secondary memory track.
—DAVID EAGLEMAN

The amygdala is like a smoke detector for the brain.
—STEPHEN JOSEPH

The air from the mattress groans when I squat to stand to answer.
Charlie, again. By the window now, my phone like a flare when I answer.

> After the crash, I dialed number by number the only number I remembered.
> Every push was a retrieval, every retrieval a removal. Every call, he answered.

My line soundless and soundless still when his voice emerges, a crocodile.
Between each bellow, a swallowing of words. *Charlie*—I tear—when I answer.

> I was fastened to the ring and rang him, like a teenager, all day. At his work,
> he was one in a chorus of concern, so raised the phone to the hall. Who answered?

Around me, a concentration of heat and me a sash window painted shut. Tonight,
he begs anew: *Who do you think you are?* With every dial, he repairs his answer.

> In the *before*—before my hardware's failure, I was not a cold computer. Before
> the paramedics, before my unceasing reboots, I left him a voice mail to answer.

Where have you gone? he wants to know. I am where I am too early: no one
from the city has come with electricity. If he searches, nowhere will answer.

> Often his line cut in the re-call. In the car, I relayed, to his music, to the freeway
> wind, my concussion. Louder then, when his windows were up: *Well, didn't I answer?*

His voice diminishes; a memory. Alone he remembers one way I loved him
eternal. Deleted now, only he knows what my last words were, and if he answered.

You there? With myself I conversed in the room where he put my disembodied
daze on speaker. His name through the hearth I replicated viral. No answer.

I rest between windows when I hear his keening move from room to hall
to street. His *Darling!* comes double in the latency; my name's not there to answer.

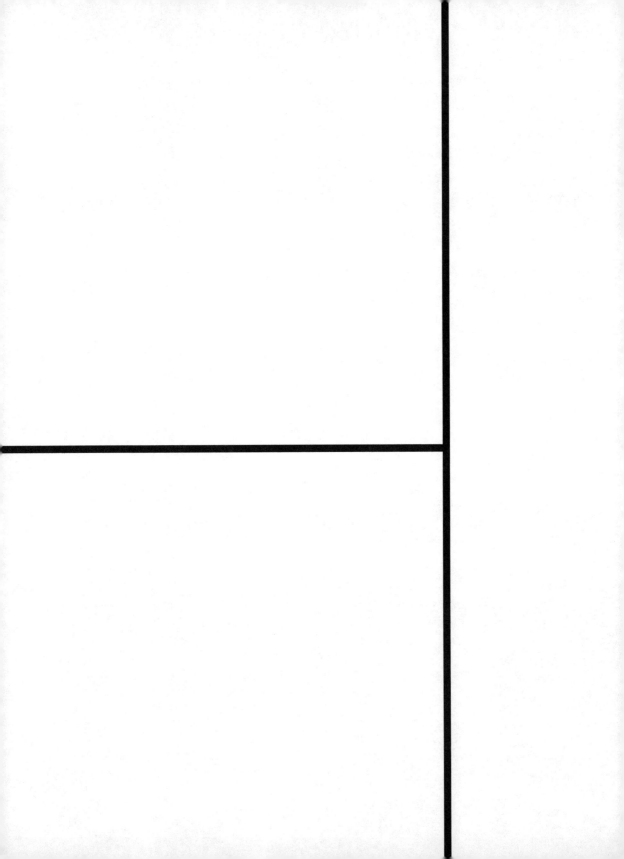

VULNERABILITY ROADSHOW

As much as we like to think we're invincible, we're not. But what if we were to change?
What if our bodies were built to survive a low impact crash? What might we look like? The
result of these questions is Graham, a reminder of just how vulnerable our bodies really are.
—TRANSPORT ACCIDENT COMMISSION VICTORIA,
Meet Graham: The Only Person Designed to Survive on Our Roads

[Twelve Apostles]

I begin the end of this life's decade with vertigo on the bluff
where everything wears you. On the limestone eroded into stacks:
your neckless monument of a head. Seven metaphors above water
while the wind speeds the waves. Always now I sense in the wrong
tense; without memories, there is only likeness.

[Legs & Feet]

A mirror image of myself on the road, I panic my way to you.
My left elbow chafes from the center console, but I orient
by pointing in the direction of every turn. You, you are spring-
loaded, hoof-footed on the frontier of what is human. Alongside
you bound, then zigzag—knee, ankle, calf, heel—into the ryegrass.

[Helmet]

For every vulnerability, the makers designed a solution—you
absorb your own motion. Your crumple-zoned head swallows
any shattering. I imagine it a mystery box our hands can
creep into on Halloween. We become charmed by yarn, tongues
of banana, grapes, and dried apricots. At what we catch, we guess.

[Face]

Daily, visitors riddle with *tumors* your name. Where I nest
in the museum, I overhear them. You are become a *Hell*
Spawn in need of a face-lift. The grotesque outhouse. Cousin you don't
talk about. "He's mine," the docent warns when I ring you.
She winks, but you are palpable enough I bite: "I *will* fight you."

[Skin]

You were cultivated like me with thick skin. At a screech,
you could eject from the windshield intact as a shard. Velvet
stanchions keep me from testing you, but blue I can see
veins your freckled and haired, counterfeit flesh. I was bruised
sore as your blue on my legs, hips, and knees. Nothing cut me.

[Skin]

Lacerations, they said, leave *lasting reminders*, so I imagine
a laceration parts my hair, not the wide-toothed comb.
I imagine a remembered life, imagine remembering.
Like a car, they poured you with the road in mind.
I imagine navigating my head to illuminate my mind.

[Brain]

In my family, Graham, we stall, make it through the Christmas
ham, the champagne and grapes at midnight of the new year,
then die. A decade ago on the eve, Graham, I slid into the halo
of radiation, not tradition. I recall an amnesiac's stillness,
plugging the stringed lights, and the canticle drumming on:

> *And he lived like me, pa rum pum pum pum*
> *Me and my Graham*
> *Me and my Graham*

[Skull]

Even they couldn't protect the tender brain, so hosed around it
cerebrospinal fluid until the skull was a pool of deep ends.

[Move Device Around Slowly to Detect Location]

In every examination room, it is the same mystery: where I am,
I do not know, in space. Grout lines, transition strips, buckled
sidewalks twist, roll, and fracture my ankles. I lift a leg and next
on the staircase I am on the landing, splayed. To my doctors
I jest a chalk outline, evidence contaminating diagnosis.

[Click and Drag]

A trauma surgeon, a crash investigation expert, and an artist
walked into a team to augment your brain, cage, skull, skin,
face, knees, neck, and legs. My riddle was culled differently:
this doctor specialized in weight loss, this doctor left me on
hold, and this doctor let me fly up, up, up—all the way home.

[Searching]

I angle and aim the interface, steer it as if a wheel at you
and, until you are found, it is me reflected, face overlaid
with the throbber:
                    (Unfortunately, 'Vulnerable' Has Stopped).

[Rib Cage]

If, to drown, I carried you beyond the sand, would you float
us back? Think *airbag rather than armour*, advised the trauma
surgeon, so they smattered your frame with sargassum weed.

If you were my passenger, would we be bedaubed in liquid
or air upon impact? If you drove and I reached to tickle you?

[Tango]

An architect reasons, *Form follows function*. To understand you,
I cannot, in this atrium, understand you without this intervening
screen. Your information delays, then fails at times in the load.
You are a *location* in the finding, and *Graham* when located. This
is the closest I have come to understanding the range of whiplash's
motion. Vibrating next door, the library renovates from the bones.

[Mirror Box Therapy]

The phantom brain pain ailed me. In dressing rooms,
I performed illusions: I made my selves three at the trifold.
Behind one mirror, I hid the bad head. Before one mirror,
I praised the good head. *Unclench*, I ordered the brain
and it hemorrhaged symmetric, a Rorschach inkblot.

[Quiz for Students]

1.   *How does* Janine's *head protect* her *brain?*
2.   *How has* Janine's *skull been engineered to protect* her *brain?*
3.   *How has* Janine's *face been designed to reduce injury in a crash?*
4.   *What has happened to* Janine's *neck and why?*

[Knees]

As a child, my mother put the tape measure in her hands
then used it to exaggerate her twist around my neck and down
to my calves. I slimmed my legs until I became a Victorian
silhouette, a daughter drawn by the bay window's light.

[Neck]

A dizziness reels when I aim: (Neck). The most assailable,
they excised yours outright. A poet must have been in the mix
to worry its slouch descending upon the decade would make
of its bearer a rough beast. Upwards to your skull they braced
you with ribs, a corseted whale in the coming of the flame.

[Plume]

I venture the landscape the morning the museum is closed.
Unlike your skyborne predecessor, you are pounds of plinth
fastened to loaf and cannot roam like me along the ropes
and connected lava caves formed again and again in a time
before you and I.

[The Science of Stopping Distances]

I convert, then solve the equation to determine how much
time the texting driver had to react before impacting me.
If the report estimated the driver was traveling 50-70 mph
on a semi-residential road, where, when my father's car hovered
through the intersection, did I lose all mind of time behind me?

[Brain]

In the dark from the street, I watch as you wait for the docent
to hit the lights—or, I imagine that you do from this country-
style porch, itself a continent in the pitch. In this town that boasts,
One place, many possibilities, we are two existing in relation
to another. Graham, you are the one survived
by me.

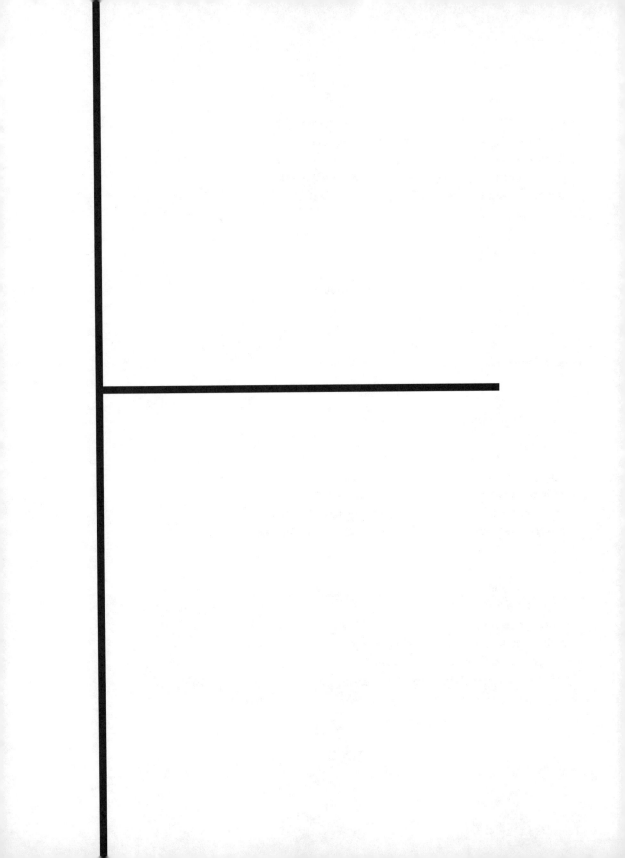

SELF-PORTRAIT WITH MEMORIES

...my life flows on, resembling life.

—OCTAVIO PAZ

ON THIS DAY   is slowly multi-tasking again.
ON THIS DAY   sleepwalks now, apparently.
ON THIS DAY   Coming and going.
ON THIS DAY   Strange, strange attraction for all things werewolf.
ON THIS DAY   is hurting more post-physical therapy.

ON THIS DAY
    My 2nd cervical vertebra slipped away (again) over
    the weekend—

ON THIS DAY   is back in California.

ON THIS DAY
    Charlie, please go back home to the person who
    has been yelling your name all day.

ON THIS DAY   is back in California.

ON THIS DAY
    *You have 3 unopened saves, including **Are you***
    forgetful? That's just your brain erasing useless
    memories.

ON THIS DAY   remembers what she did today.
ON THIS DAY   Last night, I dreamt I underwent a mastectomy.
ON THIS DAY   had a bad dream about using the wrong word.
ON THIS DAY   is in the clear. Now just waiting for her memory.

UNAUTHORIZED RISING

If on the 29th day you are born it is October
and if what your mother remembers about
your breaching is that your father
complained about the fishy smell of the
water left behind, then you may never know
when it was after the second push that you
slid into the hands of Doktora Cruel. Still
dark out, after all, is not an exact enough
minute or hour to conjure your birth chart in
the basin of the Ozarks. But ululate not
about the smeared, indecipherable script on
your birth certificate, the mayhem of their
marriage, your twelve galactic houses
shuttered up. Flex your orbs and tell me of
your suspension in the aircraft. *Time Traveler,*
Time Traveler, tell me of the cruising altitude,
of sitting open-eyed and buckled while the
day rewound. Forget you never saw your
transiting family or Pearl again. Forget the
whoosh of the sliding doors. Forget the
cover that deplaned you in the secret of
September, that bore you to this merciless
cluster. Remember your alignment of paper.
Remember the cubicle of solitude from

where you wrote your stars. *Shape-shifter,*
Shape-shifter—look now to me here. Draw
your avatars right over.

WITH AND WITHOUT CONTRAST

Though they say to lie

still, your brain can sometimes still

be a slime of what it was

if you have a night

start in the bore.

You might be

a firework

of broccoli curds, an umbrella

of orange

segments opening

on the screen.

Your brain's lit band

might bell like a pepper, *But where be*

the seeds? you will ask

because the effer

vescence

will look like danger.

A wart of garlic

a nightmare

of brussels sprouts

an onion supernova.

All of your brains

will excite

in the magnetic field.

On the narrow slab

you will

not dare close

your peach pit eyes

to the banging. And then

you'll still.

ABECEDURIAN

for Aba

Bourdain, in the rerun, says the king of fruit's Camembert-like
        custard smells of sun-spoilt death, but the phrase she recalls is

dead grandmother, which bites my tongue. How does anyone forget
        ever eating, ever excavating from the pale lobes of the foie gras

fruit, she gasps. We finish the rest of our attachment with this mis-
        giving, googling images of thorned husks bisected like my own

human brain. Impossible, to her, to sample, then overwrite the funk.
        Impossible, to her, that the Janine I was was ram-rattled into the

Janine I am now. When the concussion receded, I journeyed across
        kame and kettle in my habit of skin, immigrant again in this *after*

life of a life without my grandmother tongue. In Lake Lillian I pressed
        my forehead, but nothing natural bore me. I dub her monochrome

now with noise. *Ang Doktora, Principe Te-*
                        ñoso, Anak
                                ng Kidlat—her whole

oeuvre voiced over with what I have left. How does anyone forget?
        Pollen-yellow, the odious pulp I can't qualify on my taste buds. How

quick my mouth went dry. At the reunion, we extend the butterfly leaf,
        reminisce around the table, and in all my stories she is a monolingual

sitcom grandma. When I sketch the time she didn't know it was me
        telephoning, I flush with my hands two fluencies, the punch line

undermined. Even their memories, my memory devours into this
vanisher language. How does anyone do anything, I stop asking

when I board the plane. In this life, I exist awake until the altitude change
exhumes me. Where did she go, where did I go in that rest. I've heard it's

xenoglossy, what happened next: I heard through the pane, faint as
zodiacal light, her voice in the air beyond where the body went down.

ESSENTIALLY WITHIN NORMAL LIMITS

I observe my condition on the face of the technician who adheres
the electrodes to the scalp between my hairs. All she wonders about

me she reads from the chart: *Awake, alert and oriented x 3*. Look here,
she says, look here. She adjusts the wires until I am a plasma dome

within the recording's touch. At her direction, I move my eyelids—
open, close, open, close. *Ok, you're good,* she says, and I perform

a phenomenon of filaments. Into the wind, a dandelion wish.

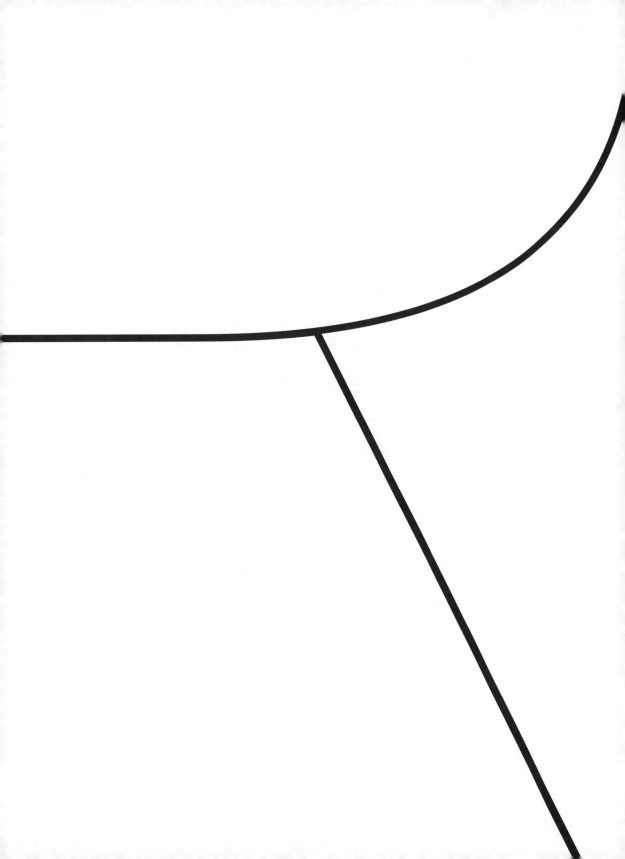

MUSCLE MEMORY

Over—before touching skin, she drapes, then touches,
        through flannel, me. Maybe, to her, I feel

dead when, over me, her hands move, through the weave,

to touch my arches, ball to heel, then up, high
        enough she must gather, like a curtain, and draw

                the table sheet back. It is not rest where I, face down,

        in the eucalyptus room, go. It is not breath she kneads
when, in me, she splits, realigns, a crossing of tissue. It is not

        her who, from me, tenses a fire, an island, then

                arcs, the length of me, knotting. Who rouses
        therapied me first—the churn of his hands that slid, then

stilled atop me, me who, in commotion within me,

        lay, like a crater, dormant. I warped, a chain she
                shakes before striking hot the stone on my upper, then

        lower back where, he confessed, he therapied to touch,

to think, when he was with his wife, of me, of my island's
        beautiful women, all alike and like its beauty. *So,*

                he said, his hands a room, glacial. *So beautiful,*

        my hardening she elbows, knuckles, then wrings. *Breathe,*
long, deep, she draws, then drapes, when I've died, my skin.

RECURRING NIGHTMARE

While you are healing, you should be very careful to avoid doing anything that could cause a bump, blow, or jolt to the head or body. On rare occasions, receiving another concussion before the brain has healed can result in brain swelling, permanent brain damage, and even death....

—CENTERS FOR DISEASE CONTROL AND PREVENTION

I keep my hinges warm. Danger is a floating
shelf, a wall cabinet door snapped and left
ajar, a shark-nose edge above a crouch.

Through the house I move in a sumo squat,
in a lunge with oblique twist, in a pulse-pulse

reverse. I duckwalk the wall and where I dip
danger dips, we bear crawl-low. On I slip

an off-road helmet and coast, round no corner
in the minefield bone-first. But ballistic I go
in my lucid dreams: I verge, then clip the fourteen-

wheelers, ramble wet into the brain's electric feel-
ers. Oh, the places this life beyond life will go!

On my haunches there I'm alive to wake;

I fetch my frights and let them detonate.

AIRBAG ARIA

Picture burnt rubber hurtled through red. That's all
I remember. Nothing and nothing but the narrative

        I've shaped of it. Of the holiday, nothing, and nothing

of the route the firefighters pried in rescue.
My father, too, fizzles when I don't remember him in

        my cycling, though he asked me from his velocity

a question I answered: *Are you okay?*
But you, I remember you—you who I heard

        never saw, but, in your careering, felt us—the least.

I named you like family in my head and let you
lap years in the fluid that buoyed me.

        Do you think of us ever, or are we as occluded by the cell light,

the chemicals and airbag that before you
deployed? Nothing appeared to halt me but the air

        and the dash. I've reveled in my study of the design:

my *stature* so small the safety system detected me
no occupant. From *the passenger seat, no occupant*

        answered my father. Imagine my being no one perhaps

saved my life or saved me from losing more
than the memory of a changed life.

        Imagine it with me. It allows me to forgive. Imagine with me

the alternative: it takes a *considerable impact*, a head-
on collision for a headstone to pillow.

Instead, I am alive with forgiveness. I forgive even the contact

who tweets about her *friends who just marry*
americans and get green cards shoved up their asses

left and right and center. You come to me when I brace for the flash

of glass—*SAD!*—
for the rear seat and trunk to send me into the belt.

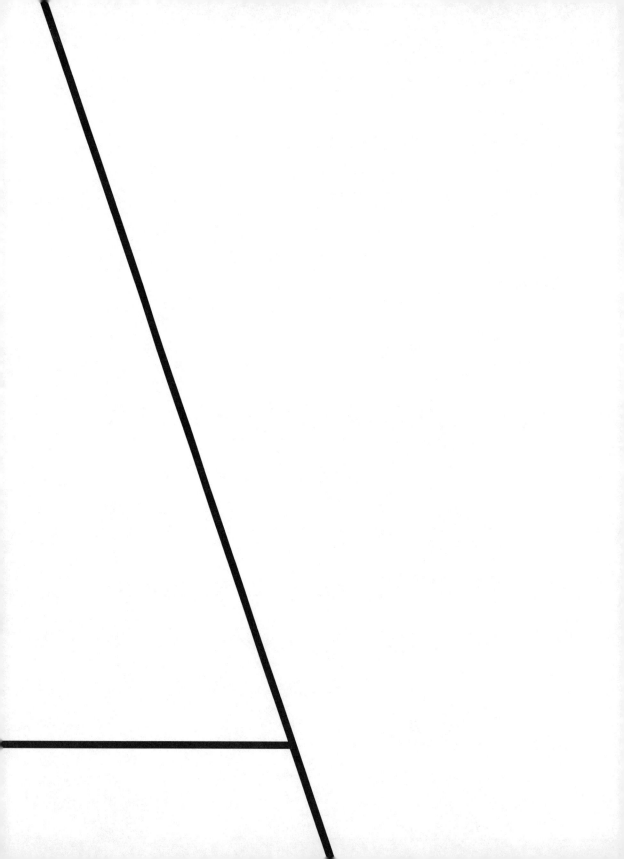

AT THE HAWTHORNE BARBELL CLUB

Memory makes demands darker than my own...
—JERICHO BROWN

Now I am sure I heard the air leave me.
Where, over the seatbelt, did my matter go?

      Where did I go, slumped over the seatbelt?
      What use is a skull if the mandible slacks?

What use is the body that cracked, in the ambulance,
comedy? Did stand-up on the gurney, into the mask.

      I gagged through my oxygen at the hospital.
      A snooze, no caregiver thought to wake me.

But in this garage, two put my rest to use.
At the rack, they load my bar with weights.

      Two by two, they clamp the bumper plates.
      At me they whoop, *Elbows down! Fight it!*

At me they whoop, *Elbows down! Fight it!*
so loud I can't hear the air heave me.

STILLWATER

With no metaphors for what turns and turns, for what
meets the ground from clouds, I collapse in the room
my barn-blue, silicone funnel. My students, as unruffled
as the spectators who they say will idle on the high-
way while the sky rotates earthward, go round the rows
with advice. I'll *survive fine* in this new city without shelter
underground, they soothe. *Get a weather radio, get yourself
a helmet.* I jot their notes verbatim so when I later walk
my beagle along the bend and glimpse—held motionless
in the reflection—a formation shaped like a beaver's tail
in the water, I don't startle, but look up to where he pulls:
at the egret, the scissortail, the range above us—swallowed!

MY CHIROPRACTOR GIVES ME A NAME

for *what's the matter:* the white

stack of vertebrae curving in

reverse in my neck in the revelatory

film. I massage my misery but cannot see

the error in what she touches

on the negative, distracted I am

by the sight of the illuminated

petroglyphs bucking beneath my

occipital bone. *We can correct this,*

she says—and she twice does

so fast I do not remember closing,

on the drop table, my eyes.

On my back, low tide and stray stars

suddenly after a decade, then her voice

pooling clear in my ears. She by the light

box where my spine lingers lets me

heave an *Oh* when I side-by-side see

a healthy neck against mine and see-see

my nape as held by the wreck. *Oh!*

she leans in her study of what of my body

the rays traveled accidentally: my costal

cartilage long calcified, skeleton a lantern

framing the air rendered black. I put my face

in the reflection.

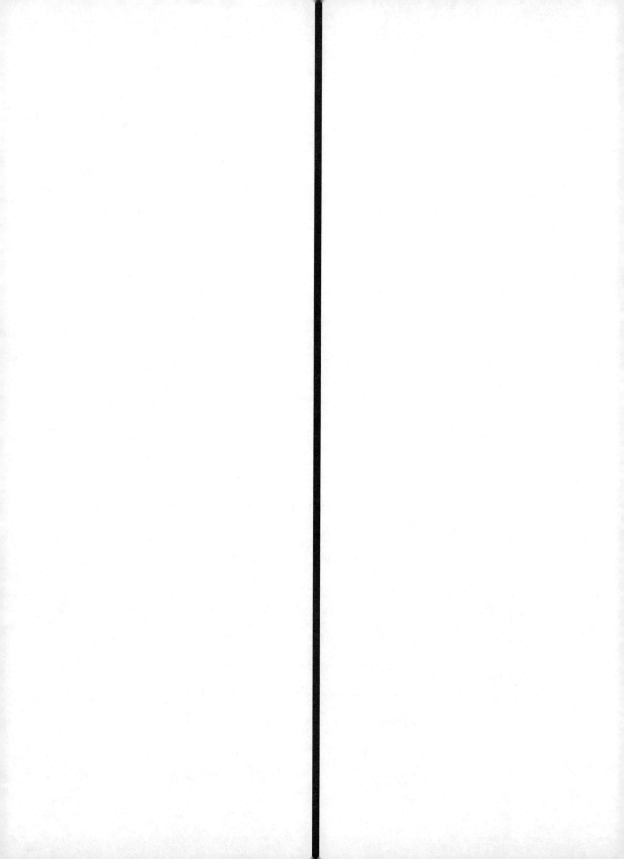

THE REVERSE OF VOLUME

I'm interested in invisible things like air, or time, or gravity, or some kind of phenomenon.

—YASUAKI ONISHI

little watering can
little watering can
my brain leaked
my brain leaked
little watering can

my brain leaked
little watering can
little watering can
my brain leaked
my brain leaked
little watering can
little watering can
my brain leaked
my brain leaked

little watering can
little watering can
my brain leaked
my brain leaked
little watering can
little watering can
my brain leaked
my brain leaked

little watering can

my brain leaked

seconds of you first

in my sleep to see if
seconds of you first
seconds of you first
in my sleep to see if
in my sleep to see if

seconds of you first
seconds of you first
in my sleep to see if
in my sleep to see if

seconds of you first
seconds of you first
in my sleep to see if

seconds of you first
seconds of you first
in my sleep to see if
in my sleep to see if

seconds of you first
seconds of you first
in my sleep to see if
in my sleep to see if
seconds of you first
seconds of you first
in my sleep to see if
in my sleep to see if

seconds of you first

in my sleep to see if

I'd awake
if I'd object
I'd awake

if I'd object
I'd awake
I'd awake
if I'd object
if I'd object

I'd awake
if I'd object
if I'd object
I'd awake
I'd awake
if I'd object
if I'd object

I'd awake

if I'd object
I'd awake
if I'd object

I'd awake
I'd awake
if I'd object
if I'd object
I'd awake
I'd awake
if I'd object
if I'd object

but it was
but it was
but it was
but it was
but it was
but it was

you—I mean—*you*
you—I mean—*you*
you—I mean—*you*
you—I mean—*you*
you—I mean—*you*
you—I mean—you
you—I mean—you
you—I mean—you
you—I mean—you
you—I mean—you
you—I mean—you

clear past

the soft archway, the island
the soft archway, the island
the soft archway, the island
the soft archway, the island
the soft archway, the island
the soft archway, the island
the soft archway, the island
the soft archway, the island
the soft archway, the island

then me following you

and me making your way
and me making your way
toward me   you
toward me   you
and me making your way

toward me   you

and me making your way
and me making your way
toward me   you
toward me   you
and me making your way
toward me   you

and me making your way
toward me   you

you

you

you   , me   where no one could see—

Maybe this is—
Maybe this is—

Is this not—
Is this not—

        I asked
        I asked

but my counselor was a specialist in grief
but my counselor was a specialist in grief
but my counselor was a specialist in grief
but my counselor was a specialist in grief
but my counselor was a specialist in grief
but my counselor was a specialist in grief

and you seemed a specter
and you seemed a specter
in my death, to her
and you seemed a specter
and you seemed a specter
in my death, to her
in my death, to her
and you seemed a specter
in my death, to her
and you seemed a specter
and you seemed a specter
in my death, to her
in my death, to her
and you seemed a specter
and you seemed a specter
in my death, to her
in my death, to her

and you seemed a specter
in my death, to her

    and she knew   only what I could tell

I was doused

drowsed
drowsed
drowsed
drowsed
drowsed
drowsed
drowsed
drowsed
drowsed
drowsed
drowsed
drowsed
drowsed
drowsed
drowsed
drowsed
drowsed
drowsed
drowsed
drowsed
drowsed
drowsed
drowsed
drowsed
drowsed
drowsed
drowsed
drowsed
drowsed
drowsed
drowsed
drowsed
drowsed
drowsed
drowsed

      for hours the bed sheet a lung
      on the rooftop billowing

         swelter binding
         swelter binding
         swelter binding
         swelter binding
         swelter binding
         swelter binding
         swelter binding

         swelter binding

   to the

drowsed

     our bodies   , the Brooklyn skyline

my hands, two   subway cars
my hands, two   subway cars
    my hands, two   subway cars
my hands, two   subway cars

lathering at the sink
running parallel

a wakening friction

in the skimming
in the skimming
in the skimming
in the skimming
in the skimming
in the skimming
in the skimming
in the skimming
in the skimming
in the skimming

in the skimming

I remembered

I remembered
I remembered

I remembered
I remembered
I remembered

I remembered
I remembered

                    you
          accelerating in swells—
               une petite

              une petite
            une petite
           une petite
              une petite
                une petite

                 une petite

one day you should know

my love had turned me open
and you were the leaf

                                        pressing nearest to my spine
                                        pressing nearest to my spine
                                        pressing nearest to my spine
                                        pressing nearest to my spine
                                        pressing nearest to my spine
                                        pressing nearest to my spine

my house was still and

from the shelf like a book

you knocked

and knocked the headboard

box fans in the window watching

                              flurry in the gallery
                              flurry in the gallery
                              flurry in the gallery
                              flurry in the gallery
                              flurry in the gallery
                              flurry in the gallery

                              flurry in the gallery

when to you I appear

do I flicker
do I flicker

   on

      a reel in the projector

           or

is it as it was   before

      simply, that I was
        that I am
        that I am
        that I am
        that I am
        that I am
        that I am

        that I am

      on your mind

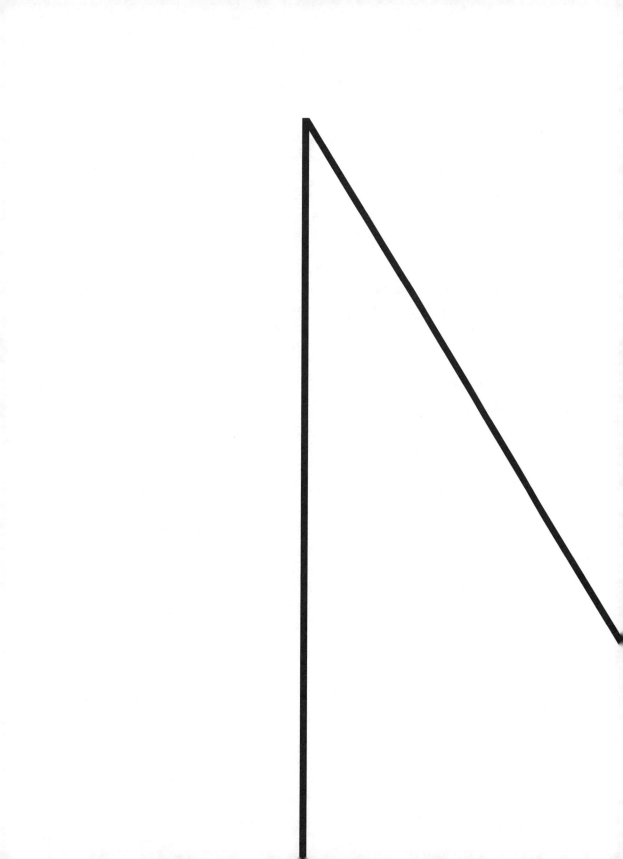

OH, I'M DYING, I'M DYING,

                              the disembodied voice ribs
in the clip of the snake whirlpooling itself to a fake death.
          Blech, she belches, *blepp*,
as the faux cobra scrapes, underside-up along the grass, forked
                              tongue trailing the coil. *Oh,*
I'm dead—but we know it's not. The touch-me-not gapes
          its mouth long enough
to be patted again by the cowgirl who runs one finger a length
                              of ventral scales. With shit
it musks itself, sometimes punctures a bleed in its commitment
          to being left alone.
I rewind to the seconds of its resurrection, when it flips to flee,
                              and pause to admire its hog-
nose of a snout, upturned and useful, subtle shovel in the plot.

HOUSE HUNTERS

Under the spindlework arch of the wraparound
        porch, no one ever thinks they'll expose
the original hardwood for its kindling. But no one

ever likes the wall-to-wall carpets, the disco granite,
        the open-concept concept. For every wish
for *character*—the toilet, sink, and clawfoot tub

a demolition green—there is an equal desire
        for *move-in ready*, for a home's lines to be
as clean as a bowl. At the bay window, a buyer

draws imaginary curtains when she says she wants
        to feel the outside when inside. Another wants
to start a family, so descends the narrowing acreage

into the basement she'll make a cave. When one
        ascends the budget, the other makes to slash
her throat with her index finger and the ruin

I imagine spills evenly across the split-level stairs.
        On the couch eating cereal, I see myself flash
on the screen gone black between cuts, and soon I too want

to gut the entryway for its potential, want to carve the suites
        until what's left is a plat of bones and my stomach full.

EPITHALAMIUM ENDING IN DIVORCE

You were bothered, I could tell, through the pomp,
the vows, their kiss's soft applause. At the late reception
of fairy lights in mason jars, you were a strobe of looks
and looked at while you tongued the open bar dry.
I held you up in the melody because you were mine
the way the country in you was mine. Two crooks
hung around my shoulders in the sway. An affection,
I could see, the way you let me see the wells grow damp.

LOVE IN THE TIME OF VERTIGO

Without help now
I can maneuver myself

upright, then supine to correct
the wind spinning my brain

from myself. My face angled
and pillow propping my shoulders,

I can hear about your day.
Though the thick tongue of air

pressures my skull under
the surface of speech,

my eyes can nod and nod.
Magnificent, the years

that have brought me here.
Once, love, I was a globe

sucked on my axis.
I was the level air bubble

some days and some days
the horizontal plane

sloping the vial. A windmill,
once, I made of my arms

and swept picture
after picture from the walls.

I was the stream of particulate
light, my love, that sheared

a home. What can I say
about what finally exits

the labyrinth?
          Sit with me while I finish

rotating my head, then
          body, and I will tell you.

THE NIGHT BEFORE YOU ARE NATURALIZED

we practice an ordinary life. Fresh off my flight,

you ask if I have eaten, and I ask you if you are hungry

and we pull into the lot of the nearest restaurant

that has something for you and something for me.

It is almost spontaneous—we just have to make

a quick call to say they can eat on ahead without us.

You are seated to face me, and, out of habit, I face

the window that overlooks the corner and reach

of street. I order what I've missed most and you

listen for what is good here, then order what comes

recommended. It takes me through the appetizers

to not be distracted by the moment's poetry, how

I might write a poem titled like that magazine's tagline—

They're Just Like Us! for example. Or a poem set here,

against the partition, where I erase you by calling you

ALIEN RELATIVE in every instance where the "you"

appears and I disappear behind THE PETITIONER

in a bit of verse not really for us but for the paparazzi

reading. I focus when I see you fumbling with your grin,

your front flipper tooth suddenly chipped in half,

which you hand me when I ask what it is that you

have done. Our dinner bowls arrive, but we are busy

rehearsing your backup face for tomorrow's pictures.

When we finally eat, a silence settles that isn't silence.

You just won't smile, you say, and show me the closed

beam you'll make, and I say I'll figure it out, don't worry,

I'll fix it. And I do—with a needle and a glue, I bond it.

DECADE OF THE BRAIN

*The boundaries of a CDP have no legal status and may not always correspond with the
local understanding of the area or community with the same name.*
        —*WIKIPEDIA, "CENSUS-DESIGNATED PLACE"*

Alone from my porch, through the tick-thick grass

            and into the street suffused with mammatus light,
I walk. No birds call, but the gale pulls chimes

from the wood. Days and nights with the movers pass

        and I make a career of anticipating
                on the buckled blacktop a tornado to descend

        like a spine and distort the field. It is mine now,

a yard among yards where neighbors hedge their cars
        crosswise and the steel blooms at solar noon. Mine,

                the salaried life my parents scrounged for, one can

        at a time in the shopping cart we raucoused
for miles down graveled roads like these.

        I can see it through the glare: Pedley, California,

                1991. My first fall in the decade of *understanding
and discovering our selves* as Americans. The little we knew

we balanced on a wobbly, folding wicker chair,

        changing the channels by hand with a knob
                until the electricity shut off and the pool scourged

with mosquitoes. Clear still, the ringing of pennies rained

from their pockets into the three-foot-tall glass jar
    centered in the home like a hearth. I can see it

        though my searches load our disappearance

    from the map. In history, we exist only in the count,
our bodies a record of a place absorbed

        by ink. But I was witness. I watched their teeth,

            their hair fall out in clenches I temper
now, here, on this plain far and away

from each of them, where decades have done nothing

    but landscape the landscape. Still, still—
        they are here as I am, landlocked

as I remember it.

NOTES

On *Decade of the Brain:* This collection and poem title borrow their name from Presidential
Proclamation 6158, which declared 1990-1999 "The Decade of the Brain." In the poem, the
italicized phrase is drawn from the title of two of its symposia: "Understanding Our
Selves: The Science of Cognition" and "Discovering Our Selves: The Science of Emotion."

Coup-Contrecoup: When referencing Odysseus, this poem echoes the orders he gave his men to tie
him to the mast as they approached the Sirens.

Epigraph: The quote attributed to Oriane Bertone, French climber and youngest to send a V14, was
received secondhand. Following a Q&A on Instagram stories, author and climber John
Burgman tweeted, "When asked about route reading and memorization, 16-year-old French
#climbing phenom Oriane Bertone said, 'My method to remember [the route] is identifying
the two or three main rest points, and repeating the moves between them like a poem'"
(7/11/21).

Four Darks in Red: The title is borrowed from the Mark Rothko painting of the same name.

Circuitry: In this poem, the speaker sings a phrase from "Just Dance" by Lady Gaga.

Erasure: This poem is also a found poem, with the source text drawn in large part from a
neurological consultation I had a year and a half after the 2008 accident. Besides folders and

envelopes of medical bills and insurance invoices, it remains one of the few documents I have chronicling that period of my life.

The Specialists: This poem borrows "commotion" from within the definition of cerebral concussions, as penned by neurosurgeon Benjamin Bell in 1787: "Every affection of the head attended with stupefaction, when it appears as the immediate consequence of external violence, and when no mark or injury is discovered, is in general supposed to proceed from commotion or concussion of the brain, by which is meant such a derangement of this organ as obstructs its natural and useful functions, without producing such obvious effects on it as to render it capable of having its real nature ascertained by dissection."

Janine vs Janine: This poem draws from mischief depicted in the complete first season of *Spy vs Spy* on MAD TV (available in its entirety on YouTube). It was also written with its ear pressed to the season's theme music. In its latter half, the poem makes reference to the lying, passing, and hiding that Jose Antonio Vargas writes "all undocumented immigrants experience" in his memoir, *Dear America: Notes of an Undocumented Citizen.*

Near the End of Our Time: The italicized text comes from the leaflet, "How to Do Progressive Muscle Relaxation," published by Anxiety Canada™.

Vulnerability Roadshow: In 2018, I received a grant to see Graham at the Hamilton Gallery in Hamilton, VIC, Australia. The exhibition featured an interactive, life-size sculpture of an "evolved" human form designed to survive a low impact car crash. Thinking deeply about what changes a person might undergo in order to survive a life-altering event, the creative team—comprised of Transport Accident Commission Victoria, a trauma surgeon, a crash investigation expert, and Melbourne-based artist Patricia Piccinini—culled medical data to augment Graham's brain, face, skull, face, neck, rib cage, skin, knees, and legs. The poem draws details from the exhibit, as well as from the educational resource guide available online ("Meet Graham: Teaching and Learning Ideas"). Its title also borrows from language used in the manual for museum docents (thank you again for sharing these with me). Phrases in [Face] and [Neck] echo moments from Tennyson's "Ulysses" and Yeats's "The Second Coming," respectively.

Self-Portrait with Memories: This is a found poem, comprised of Facebook Memories from 2008-2018.

Unauthorized Rising: The lyrics of the Red Rover game are mimicked when the Time Traveler and Shape-shifter are conjured.

With and without Contrast: Images within the poem are inspired by MRI technologist Andy Ellison's "Inside Insides" project.

Abecedurian: Lillian Leonardo, my grandmother who we called Aba, was a well-known actress who starred in numerous films for Sampaguita Pictures in the Philippines. This poem also uses the 28-letter Filipino alphabet that I grew up with, which includes the letters ñ and ng.

Recurring Nightmare: In the dipping sequence, the poem momentarily grooves to Freak Nasty's "Da' Dip." Later, it riffs to *Oh, the Places You'll Go!* by Dr. Seuss.

Airbag Aria: Regarding airbags, the U.S. National Highway Traffic Safety Administration reports, "Many advanced frontal air bag systems automatically turn off the passenger air bag when the vehicle detects a small-stature passenger or child, a child in a child restraint system, or no occupant in the right front passenger seat."

At the Hawthorne Barbell Club: This poem is for Molly and Morgan.

The Reverse of Volume: This poem takes its title from and is inspired by Yasuaki Onishi's mountainous, reverse sculpture installation, *reverse of volume RG.*

ACKNOWLEDGMENTS

Thank you to the editors and staffs of the following publications where these poems first appeared, sometimes in different versions:

Academy of American Poets' *Poem-a-Day* series: "Circuitry" and *"Oh, I'm Dying, I'm Dying,"*

The Adroit Journal: "Into the Ganzfeld" (as "The Part of the Water")

The Arkansas International: "Every Good Boy Does Fine"

Copper Nickel: "Near the End of Our Time,"

The Cortland Review: "Epithalamium Ending in Divorce"

The Georgia Review: "In the Ecotone"

MumberMag: "Love in the Time of Vertigo"

The Nation: "House Hunters"

Orion Magazine: "Stillwater"

Pleaides: Literature in Context: "American Sentences" and "Coup-Contrecoup"

Poetry Northwest: "The Night before You Are Naturalized"

Quarterly West: "The Persistence of Symptoms"

The Rumpus: "My Chiropractor Gives Me a Name"

Sixth Finch: "Airbag Aria" and "Love, Elizabeth"

Waxwing (two issues): "Abecedurian," "Erasure," "Four Darks in Red," "How to Explain My Becoming (as "Cerebral Edema"), "Muscle Memory," "Unauthorized Rising," and "With and without Contrast" (as "Reading the Bleed")

World Literature Today: "Intake Form" (as "New Patient Intake Form") and "You Lose Your Keys, Too, and"

"The Persistence of Symptoms" was reprinted on the Academy of American Poets website.

"Four Darks in Red" was developed as a limited edition broadside, designed by Gabrielle Bates, for Bull City Press.

Special thanks to Camonghne Felix for selecting "My Chiropractor Gives Me a Name" as the finalist for The Poetry Society of America's 2021 Lyric Poetry Award.

"After the Flood," a poem originally published by the now-defunct *La Fovea*, was stripped for parts to build other poems in the book. The poem had previously won a 2010 Brazos Bookstore/Academy of American Poets Prize, selected by Laura Kasischke.

"Self-Portrait around the Bends" contains material that originally appeared in my essay "Recovery," published in *The Poem's Country: Place & Poetic Practice* (Pleiades Press, 2018). Shara Lessley, thank you for working with me on the essay and for making it feel like I could write this book at all.

The completion of this book would not have been made possible without the time, space, instruction, camaraderie, and generous financial support from Bethany Arts Community; College of Arts and Science and Department of English at Oklahoma State University; Hedgebrook; Inprint; Kundiman; MacDowell; Sewanee Writers' Conference; Telitha E. Lindquist College of Arts & Humanities at Weber State University; and The Writers' Colony at Dairy Hollow. A special thanks to Robin, Jeannine, and Jana for keeping my brain fed. Blake, for reminding me to be brave.

My ability to write this book was also supported in part by a grant from the Paul and Daisy Soros Fellowship for New Americans. The Fellowship gave my brain time to assemble itself. The program is not responsible for the views expressed in this book.

Tonya, Durandi, Steven, and Dani—thank you for visiting me in the days after the accident.

Aba, thank you for watching over us those first nights. To my family, thank you.

Thank you to my teachers, colleagues, and peers at the University of Houston Creative Writing Program—especially all on the listserv who witnessed my concussion symptoms in real time.

Thank you to my Kundiman family—especially all on OpenSpace who witnessed my concussion symptoms in real time. Kundiman is forever. Thank you to Eugene Gloria, Patrick Rosal, and Arthur Sze—your prompts at the Retreat stirred this book's beginnings.

Endless thanks to Alice James Books for welcoming me back home. Thank you to Alyssa Neptune for your constant guidance and Julia Bouwsma for your attentive eye. Carey Salerno, thank you for believing in this book and trusting in my vision of it—in many ways, you set this material free.

Thank you to foam rollers, TENS units, racquetballs for trigger points, extra-large gel ice packs, heating pads, dry needles, and the Hypervolt. Thank you to the nurses, doctors, physical therapists, massage therapists, acupuncturists, chiropractors, neurologists, therapists, psychologists, and neuropsychologists who were gentle with me through the years.

Thank you to my Undocupoets—all and all to come—for, in the words of Toni Morrison, continuing to claim the edge as central and "let the rest of the world move over to where (we are)."

Sojourner Ahébée, T. J. Anderson III, Julie and Scott Bear Don't Walk, Paul Hlava Ceballos, Cathy Linh Che, Olin Caprison, Larin Davis, Will Donnelly, Lisa Sanaye Dring, Laura Eve Engel, Marina Fridman, Aja Gabel, Clemonce Heard, Hilal Isler, Ndinda Kioko, Joseph O. Legaspi, Elizabeth Lyons, Diane and Jennifer Mitchell, Rajiv Mohabir, Nita Noveno, Soham Patel, Kevin Prufer, Iliana Rocha, Matthew Salesses, Analicia Sotelo, Lara Stapleton, Wolfcat, Erin Wood, Jenny Xie, and my multi-month MacDowell cohort: thank you for your friendship, gifs, dog photos, rehabilitation, and care that have tethered me. Rosalie Moffett and TC Tolbert, thank you for those pockets of conversations about accident aftermaths. Mihaela Moscaliuc—thank you for your foresight.

Thank you to John Murillo and R. A. Villanueva, who know me from *the before* and who continue to remind me who I am. Ron, thank you especially for remaining on the "i think i was in an accident"-loop with me.

Sarah Beth Childers, thank you for riding these book years alongside me. Marci Calabretta Cancio-Bello, thank you for your love and tsismis, and for enduring years of poem drafts sent via screenshot, via text. Who would I be without you, Scully? Thank you for carefully reading my discharge papers and sending me back to the doctor.

And—always and always—thank you to Eric and Bartleby for *the after*.